WORDS OF WISDOM
FOOD FOR THOUGHT

Words Of Wisdom
Food For Thought

Nancy F. Artis

Kravitz & Sons
INNOVATORS IN PUBLISHING, MARKETING AND ADVERTISING

Kravitz and Sons LLC
1301 Farmville Blvd, Suite 104
Greenville, NC 27834

Published by Kravitz and Sons LLC.

ISBN: 979-8-89639-218-7 (sc)
ISBN: 979-8-89639-219-4 (e)

Library of Congress Control Number: 2025905496

CONTENTS

INTRODUCTION

Words of Wisdom, Food for Thought is a collection of spiritual passages that renews and strengthens. You are reminded to trust the infinite wisdom of your spiritual being to guide you. As you read, trust your divine self is following a path toward peace, joy, and the blessings of a Heavenly Being.

BLACK IS...

Beautiful
Soulful
Very bold

Black is:
Friendly
Kind
Nice to have on your mind.

MY JOURNEY

Many twists and turns
The who, what, where, and why of life
The presence of Spirit all around
A time to meditate with self
One day at a time

BLACK IS TO BLACK

Happy
Out of Sight
Glad
Fine
Proud
Beautiful
Just like a Petunia Pad...
Black is what I don't mind Being!

GOD IS...

Life:
Alpha, Omega
All and everything begins and end with God
Seasons:
Spring, Summer, Winter, Fall
The renewal of the Mind, Soul, Body, Spirit
My All and All
What Is God to You?

DEATH

Quick, Piercing
Arch Enemy
Bearer of Grief
Pain, Anguish
Opens to All
Death

DEATH

Enemy of mine and thee...
Quick to come,
Quick to take,
No Questions Asked
Simply... It's Your Time

DEATH...

Deep = Dark = Pensive
No Baggage Necessary
No Reservation
No Hesitation
Hallow Like a Shallow Well
Payment for Ones Toil—a place in the soil
Death

DEAR GOD, GOOD MORNING

Your Presence quiets the mind and
allows Your Voice to be heard.
Speak to me... I am quiet
I listen
You speak
I hear in the quiet of a moment
You are always with me and thee

SILHOUETTE OF DEATH

Shadows of gloom appear
Footprints etched with a marking for each soul
Cold dark, callous
Death appears at the end of Life's
Journey for one and all...

FOOTPRINTS

I take a step...
You take a step...
Our Footprints are here
One step at a time
Traveling from Place to Place
No Prints are identical—
Different in size, shape, and depth—
Each is Unique—
Footprints.
Mine, Yours, Ours
Cover the Earth

ODE TO A BLACK CHILD...

Black is the color of your skin
Be proud...
Own It...
Respect It...
You are here for a reason—
A season
A lifetime
Leave a Legacy for the next
Black Child

MOMENTS OF QUIET

Think
Reflect
Bless
Plan
Evaluate!

BLACK CHILD

You are born in a world full of Scorn
You will know hatred as well as Love
Meet the dawn of each day like a Dove
Rise above the turmoil
Sink your feet in the soil...

MY MAMA SAID...

I am special
I have Ebony skin
Smooth, Dark, Radiant
Mama said,
"Be Proud
You are dark ebony wood
You shine
You come from the Best..."
Mama Said,
"You are Loved as you are,
My Ebony Baby."

THE QUESTION IS

How do I live a life of Spirituality?

1. Begin each day with your spiritual being
2. Remember to forgive
3. Be thankful
4. Keep a positive attitude
5. Eliminate the negative
6. Communicate with your spiritual
being throughout your day
7. Allow yourself the joy of living a spiritual life
8. Declare Divine order in all areas of your life

Serenity Prayer

God grant me the serenity to accept
The things I cannot change
Courage to change the things I can
and wisdom to know the difference.
Living one day
At a time accepting hardships as the
Pathway to peace taking as he did this sinful
world as it is not as I would have it;
trusting that he will make things right if I surrender
to his will that I may be reasonably happy in this life
and supremely happy with him
forever in the next. Amen.

9. Remember the Serenity Prayer by Reinhold Niebuhr (1892 – 1971)
10. Remember you are never alone
11. Expect the best
12. Pray your way through all and everything
13. Remember to clothe yourself in Gods armor

I AM WOMAN

A mother
A Daughter
A Sister
A Caregiver
A creation of God with Many attributes
A celebration of Life
I am Blessed...
I Am Woman

DIVINE ORDER

Set the tone, affirm divine order
in all areas of your life.
Know and consider that things work together.
Remember the mind can declare divine
order, but your heavenly Father is in
charge and controls the steps.

NANCY'S ANGEL

My Heavenly Father has sent a Guardian
Angel to watch over me.
A Guardian Angel to guide me through
the hustle and bustle of life.
A Guardian Angel to light my way
and eliminate negative thinking.
A Guardian Angel who comforts me
and lets me know I am loved.

CLOSE THE DOOR

Let the light of God Shine in.
Cast out all hurt and pain from the past.
It's time to move forward
Leave Doubt and worry in the Past.
Open the door to the dawn of a new day.
The Light brings Joy, Peace, and Love.

TOMORROW

Enjoy the precious gifts of the Here and Now.
No need to borrow thoughts of the future.
Let tomorrow take care of itself.
You can only live one day at a time.
Why bring sorrow into today?
Rejoice in the present.
The future is in the Hands of our Heavenly Father.
Find comfort in the Lord's word:
Continue to praise and meditate on his word.
Select a Bible of choice and read from it daily.
Reference: Psalms 23:1, 91:1, 121:1, 125:1
The Holy Bible
King James Version
Thomas Nelson Publishers
Nashville
Copyright 1984, 1977
By Thomas Nelson, INC.

MORNING PRAYER

Heavenly Father,
Mother Spirit,
Good Morning, I am grateful to
begin this day with you.
You have blessed and prepared me for a new day.
You clothed me in your Divine
armor and my path is clear.
I can go forth with your abiding
peace. My day is Blessed.

MY PRAYERS FOR COMFORT

Psalm 23:1, "The lord is my
shepherd, I shall not want."
Psalm 91:1, "He that dwelleth in the
secret place of the most High
shall abide under the shadow of the Almighty"
Psalm 121:1, "I will lift up mine eyes unto
the hills from whence cometh my help."
Psalm 125:1, "They that trust in the Lord
shall be as mount Zion, which cannot
be removed, but abideth forever.

MIDDAY PRAYER

Oh, Heavenly Father, Mother
Spirit, I graciously thank you
for preparing my way for the glory
of the midday prayer.
I break now, to give praise and
thanksgiving for all and everything.
The morning prayer has unlocked
the door for our father's grace.
Be blessed. Your path is clear.

A SPIRITUAL CONNECTION

Prayer is our spiritual connection that unlocks
The door to our heavenly father or whatever name
we have for our creator.
We are Christians, but we may or
may not serve the same God.
Does it matter? No, we all pray to
the source of our Divinity
So, let's keep sending praises. We are connected
to the source; our prayers are heard.

EVENING PRAYER

Dear Heavenly Father,
The day has come to an end.
I thank thee, for bringing me forward in your favor
You have blessed my going and coming.
You have kept me safe and
surrounded by your angels.
I am guided through the storms
of life and blessed with
a grateful heart.
Thank you, my Heavenly Father
and Spiritual Mother.

THE POWER OF FAITH

Faith is the Spiritual connection that
speaks to us, the voice of our
Heavenly father saying, "My child, you
are never alone, keep your hand
in mind, for I am in you, we will always be
together, here on earth and in heaven."
What a blessing… the power of Faith.
Believe

APPOINTMENT WITH GOD

Oh, child of God, make yourself ready
No need for fancy clothes,
diamonds, gold, and silver.
Come as you are. All you need is
faith and a grateful heart
Are you ready for your appointment?

SPRING

Spring is a joyful season, a time of change
The reason for flowers to grow and glow
in various colors, sizes, and shapes.
The sound of birds chirping and squirrels
squirting up and down trees and
An array of butterflies escaping their cocoons.
We know spring has sprung and
the gloom of winter is gone.

PEACE

May the divine spirit of our Heavenly Father
Grant you peace at all times, in any situation.
God Bless.

PRAYING TIME

Heavenly Father, as I kneel in prayer, I give
praise, as I am thankful for my blessings:
Good health
A joyful heart
Peace of mind
Prosperity
Goodwill toward others
Heavenly Father, you have kept me.
I am forever in your care
AMEN.

ABOUT THE AUTHOR

Nancy Artis is a retired educator from New York City with thirty-seven plus years of experience in teaching and administration. She is the co-author of World Cultures and Geography (Grade 7), Center for Learning Publication (1987), John Carroll University, Ohio.